Sold Or Saved?

Orphans Tell Their Own Stories
of Abandonment, Torture, and Redemption

By Philip Cameron
As told to Mary Hutchinson

03282IN

Published by HigherLife Development Services, Inc.
400 Fontana Circle
Building 1—Suite 105
Oviedo, Florida 32765
(407) 563-4806
www.ahigherlife.com

Unless otherwise indicated, Bible quotations are taken
from the New International Version 1984.

ISBN 13: 978-1-939183-20-0
ISBN 10: 1939183200

First Edition 12 13 14 15 — 9 8 7 6 5 4 3 2 1

Cover Design:
Thomjon Borges

Copy Editing:
Brian Paterson, Mary Frediani and Melanie Gray

Dedication

To Stella:

*I knew you were handicapped. I knew you were orphaned.
I never thought someone would sell you and use you until you were
dead. I am so sorry I didn't keep you from this nightmare. I am so
sorry you died alone. Never again will this happen to an orphan
God brings into my life if I can help it. I promise you that.*

Philip Cameron

Acknowledgements

To all the "former orphans" in my life, I say thank you.
This is your story, not mine.

Table of Contents

Introduction

"Command those who are rich in this present world not to be arrogant nor to put their hope in wealth, which is so uncertain, but to put their hope in God, who richly provides us with everything for our enjoyment. Command them to do good, to be rich in good deeds, and to be generous and willing to share. In this way they will lay up treasure for themselves as a firm foundation for the coming age, so that they may take hold of the life that is truly life."
(1 Timothy 6:17-19, NIV)

"Have you ever seen a baby freeze to death?"

The question stopped me in my tracks as I entered the state-run orphanage for the first time on December 6, 1996. I couldn't believe what the director was asking. I looked at him dumbfounded.

Before I could respond, he continued, "We have already had sixteen babies freeze to death this year, and it is not even officially winter yet."

An uncomfortable silence fell between us. The bitter cold seeped through my thick winter coat and wool sweater and into my bones. It didn't matter that I was inside the orphanage; I was shaking uncontrollably from the chill.

The ugly grey square building I was standing in had been built to house over 100 children. Cold air rushed in from gaping holes in the windows all around me. There were dozens upon dozens of broken or missing panes with only a pitiful few patched by nothing more than flimsy newspapers, plastic bags, and tape.

A single dim bulb hanging overhead provided the only light in the room. Looking past the director, I could see the children in the shadows. From under layers and layers of clothing, their little eyes peeked up at me. It looked as if each child had put on every item of clothing they could find. Nothing fit, nothing matched, and nothing was clean.

Looking from one sad face to the next, my heart broke. These children were all painfully thin, pale beyond words, and I could tell from their runny noses that they were all sick. It was surreal, like a scene from a movie.

The director took me on a tour of the building and what I saw was mind numbing. How could anyone treat children like this?

I was told the children slept two or three to a bed, huddled together under cheap, threadbare blankets to find some warmth. There was often no food at all for days at a time. Many of the workers were cruel and heartless, berating the children, stealing the few small gifts some charity or church might bring by.

The only bathroom was as awful as any I had ever seen—it looked like it hadn't been cleaned in years, and the stench brought tears to my eyes. It didn't matter that the toilets didn't work; the children had to use them anyway. On the rare occasion the showers worked, the water came out in a cold dribble.

That day began the second chapter in my life caring for orphans.

Standing in the cold orphanage, I made a pledge to God that not one more child would freeze to death in this place. Before I left town that night, I emptied my wallet, buying enough coal to keep the children warm for a few weeks.

The next day we were back, working for hours patching windows with anything we could find. We left days later with the windows somewhat patched and a promise to the children that we'd be back soon.

This was my introduction to Moldova and the plight of the orphans there—children who looked like they could be mine, with their fair skin, high cheekbones, and piercing eyes.

My work with children had started seven years before when the Iron Curtain of Communism had fallen, and the Western World had seen the plight of the orphans in nearby Romania for the first time.

Perhaps you remember those newscasts, seeing hundreds of starving infants crammed in warehouses filled with rusted metal cribs. Naked, starving, and neglected, these babies became so engraved in my heart that I worked for years making each run-down orphanage in that country habitable.

Against all odds, one Romanian boy, a fragile four-year-old named Andrew, became my adopted son.

For me, Andrew became a symbol of all orphans in the former

Soviet bloc. Here in my comfortable American home, my wife Chrissie and I watched him grow. From the moment he was ours, his stomach never grumbled with the gnawing pains of hunger again and we loved him as much as we loved our own biological children.

But he also became a constant reminder of all of the children we had left behind. I became a driven man, determined to help care for as many of these forgotten children as possible.

How could I look in his eyes each day and forget the babies we had left behind?

The government neither wanted to care for these children, nor were they any good at it. To them, the children were nothing but a burden, and everything I saw underscored the resentment that the people felt toward these innocent orphans. I worked all across Romania for years, spending hundreds of thousands of dollars until conditions were markedly improved.

When I felt that conditions had improved enough to move on, I left Romania and traveled one country over—to a place few people have even heard of.

Moldova. A country of four million that had once been part Romania, once been part of Russia, now independent and almost as helpless as her orphans. It was the poorest country in all of Europe.

Soon after my first visit to Moldova, I started regularly bringing coal to the orphanage, installing new windows, and helping fix the leaky roofs. True to my word, with God's help, not one child ever froze there again. I filled pantries with food, dug new wells, supplied clothing, boots, and more.

I brought the first Christmas gifts these children had ever received: little toys, warm mittens, and hard candies. To pay for it all, I spoke in churches across the US to raise money. Then, I would jump on a plane and help as many children as I could before the money ran out. Then the cycle would begin again.

When the first orphanage I found was transformed, I thought my work in this country was done. Then I discovered another orphanage in a Moldovan village called Cupcui.

It was almost Christmas and, as I walked in, I heard the children singing carols to one another. It was the saddest thing I had ever seen. No gifts. No tree. No parents. The only gift they had to give each other was music.

As I listened, God said to my heart, "Don't just bring these kids stuff. Make these kids your children. Be their Dad."

"Be their Dad?!" I asked the Lord.

Bringing gifts and replacing windows, that was one thing. But being their Dad? As they say in Scotland, that is a different kettle of fish.

I said nothing to those I was with, and continued to take in the now all too familiar horror that these children called home.

Several feet of snow covered the ground outside and the flat roof above. As heat escaped through the building's poorly designed roof, snow melted, and a steady stream of water poured inside the building, soaking the thin cots the children slept on.

"When it rains for a day out there, it rains for a week in here," the director explained.

"Well," I thought, "that explains the black mold covering the walls."

As I looked around, the enormity of what God was saying jolted me to the core. Being a dad is a lifetime commitment. To be a real dad, I couldn't bounce in and out of the children's lives; I had to be there.

Yet, how could I look into the faces of these children and not do everything in my power to help them even more?

Yes, we fixed that orphanage up, too. But I had to do far more. To be their dad, I had to know these kids personally, their stories, their fears. I had to encourage them in school, in life. I had to invest much more of my time with them.

So I stepped up my visits. Chrissie and I even bought a little house down the street where I could take a half dozen children at a time to give them a weekend away from the orphanage, shower them with affection and special treats, and give them some quality time with my wife and me.

As we helped these children with their studies, as we played games with them and shared Jesus with them, they became our dearest friends.

When I was in America, I thought of the orphans day and night, fretting over each one, the stories each had shared, the nightmares all of them lived.

Then one day I learned the saddest, most sickening thing: on the first of June after their 16th birthdays, all orphans—including "mine"— are tossed on the streets. These kids have only a ninth-grade education, no family, no future, and not the skills to even boil an egg. And yet, they are abandoned, tossed out on the streets alone.

These former orphans were not nameless, faceless children to me. These were *my children* they were talking about. My children would be tossed on the streets. And what awaited them was a fate far worse than death.

In a nation known as the engine of sex trafficking for all of Europe, these orphans become the single easiest target. Over 400,000 girls and women have simply vanished.

Of those 400,000 women, one orphan, a handicapped girl named Stella that I had come to love in the first home I had visited in Moldova, was trafficked. Used over and over again, she died alone at the age of 19 from HIV.

The day I learned of her fate, it was like my heart had been crushed in my chest. I hurt so much that I couldn't breathe. Stella?

My precious Stella?

In my grief, I promised God I would make a place for every orphan in Moldova that needed a place to stay.

When we opened our first home for girls just like this one, we called it Stella's House. Today, there are 50 girls at Stella's House, and 15 in a boys' home called Simon's House.

I pray you will take the time to read some of their stories in the pages of this book.

After we built Stella's House 1, we moved on to Stella's 2, and we are now working on Stella's Houses 3 and 4. As soon as the first two Stella's Houses were full, we got some news.

The government of Moldova had made the decision that they could no longer afford to care for the 12,500 orphans in their charge. The laws in this former communist state do not allow any other organization to have an orphanage, so they got creative in how to deal with the "problem."

They bribed any relatives they could find to take in these children. I heard them tell of one drunken grandfather who took in two children in exchange for 15 chickens. One woman took her child back so she could get a kitchen table. Another worked a deal for some whitewash paint. None of these adults wanted these children.

Predictably, things did not go well for those placed.

Many of the children had been beaten. Some had run away. Four of the girls were pregnant—each between the ages of 14 and 16. They had nowhere to go. These girls were enough to cause the government to try another new approach.

But this one...it was really God's idea.

The government of Moldova asked us to take over the orphanage— the very same building in Cupcui that we had rehabbed years ago, and re-open it. It's free to us to house orphans for 25 years.

Today, this home we call Providence House is filled with children from birth to age 16. They are some of the happiest children on earth.

This book is a collection of stories from the orphans in our care. Not every story has a happy ending. As you read them, you will cry and you will feel anger, but I promise you, you will also feel hope. You will see how a little help and a big God can change the life of a child.

In these pages, you'll meet girls from Stella's House, boys from Simon's House and a few of the younger children from Providence House.

Please...keep reading.

The Girls of Stella's House

"If anyone has material possessions and sees his brother in need but has no pity on him, how can the love of God be in him? Dear children, let us not love with words or tongue but with actions and in truth."

(**1 John 3:17-18,** NIV 1984)

Natalie

Natalie C.
Orphaned at age of 7
Age today: 21

My name is Natalie.

When I was only four, my mom became blind after an accident. I remember the day she became blind because she was touching me all over my body because she couldn't recognize me. But at that age I didn't understand what happened to her and I was scared that she would never remember me.

After that, my grandma took me to her place. After a while they took me to a place in Chisinau so I could stay there and live for a while with some people. They were Christians and they wanted to adopt me and my grandma didn't want to let them adopt me and lose me forever, so she came and took me back home.

She had no money for food and struggled to keep us alive. When I was seven, she put me in the orphanage. I remember the first day at the orphanage, I saw so many kids around me so I said, "Here is going to be a fun place, I'm going to have friends."

At the beginning the teachers were nice, but they started to beat us and call us bad words and they would say, "Your mother is an alcoholic and your father is like this and like that and why should we keep you here? It's not our job to take care of you. You're nothing and you'll always be nothing."

I've never known anything about my dad. I've never known who he is. I'll always wonder, does he ever even ask about me or does he know who I am, does he know about me, does he care if I am hungry or alone?

Every Saturday for nine years, I waited at the orphanage gate watching for somebody to come and visit me and for nine years, nobody came.

I was thinking, "You are nobody, your parents don't want to come see you and you'll always be a nobody and nobody will ever want to love you. You were born but nobody really knows that you are in this world and nobody really cares about you."

Finally, I lost my hope because my mom had a boyfriend and he had two kids in the same orphanage. My mom would come to visit them but she never came to see me.

When I was 16, I knew I had to leave the orphanage in June and I didn't know where to go. I wanted to continue my studies. I wanted to show everyone in my family that I could become someone. I didn't know where to go because I didn't have any support from my family because they couldn't afford to take care of themselves.

Then, Philip Cameron came to our orphanage and changed the windows and everything. It was really great because the kids were going to have a warm place during the winter. I remember how long those nights were when we didn't have good windows and we would have to wake up in the middle of the night and try to keep the windows shut.

I said, "That is great and I wish I could stay longer in this orphanage."

As terrible as it was, in other ways, it was like my home, even if I didn't feel love. For me, it was the only place.

Philip said that he built a house for girls just like me and he said that

I could come and continue my studies. He said that I could go and visit and if I liked it, I could stay.

I remember my first day at Stella's House. We came for a visit and they made sandwiches for us. Everyone smiled and hugged us and loved on us. That was the first time I felt welcome somewhere and we didn't feel like people wanted to get rid of us.

We wanted to take our shoes off when we came in the door, but Philip said, "No, just come as you are because this is your place, it's your house."

We were so amazed that somebody could actually do that for us. We were so thankful, and I didn't believe that I could be in a house like that.

I remember staying in my bed at Stella's House and thinking how blessed I am, how God found me, and how many doors He opened in my life. All the pain that I went through, He made me a stronger person. He cared for me when I thought that nobody cared and He saw me when I thought that nobody saw me. He built me the way He wants me to be and I am so thankful for the life that I had because I wouldn't be the person that I am today if I had had a better life.

At Stella's House I went to finish my high school. At first I was afraid and ashamed to tell the other students that I was an orphan because I had so many people reject me in my life and I just had enough of it. I wanted my friends and everyone around me just to love me and accept me the way I am.

At Stella's House, I found that. I found people that loved me and cared for me and accepted me just as I was. The man I came to call Dad (Philip) taught me about God and about His love. At first I didn't understand it because I didn't know how someone could love me so much, because I am such a sinner and still God cares for me every day. He has a great plan even when I don't deserve it. I couldn't understand it, because if my mom didn't love me, why should God love me?

Dad said, in the most simple way, "On the right hand is you, and on the left hand is Jesus, and God took you and gave Jesus and God said, 'and I will give my only Son to keep you in my hand.'" That was the first time I really understood how much God loves me that He gave everything for me and that's when I accepted His love.

It was hard to trust people, and it took a while to trust my new Dad and Mom (Chrissie) and the girls and everything. I never thought that God would take away the pain from my heart like He did and at the same time, keep it fresh so I won't forget where I come from.

If it wasn't for Stella's House, I don't know where I would be today. Probably I would never know about God and I would be trafficked somewhere like other girls. I am so thankful for people around the world because they care for us.

I am so thankful to have sisters at Stella's House, just to watch them grow and become women of God and to see the pain that they went through fading away every single day. To see God working in their lives and to see that they don't become selfish but they want to give more and want to help more girls and boys just like them. That's the greatest gift, and the greatest transformation that I have ever had.

Also, I am so thankful to live in a world where all of the people around me talk about God. To be able to go back to my family and to not have any hate towards them, just forgiveness, and to want them to realize that God loves them. I don't hate my mom. I love her, even though she put me away. I am thankful that she put me in an orphanage because that's where God found me.

Galina

Galina T.
Orphaned at age of 4
Age today: 23

My name is Galina.

I was put in the Cupcui Orphanage when I was four years old. There were five brothers and sisters in my family. But my parents divorced, and my mom took some of my siblings, and my father took the others.

But me, they left in a horrible orphanage in Moldova.

I was so little when they left me that I do not remember my parents' faces at all. They have never called or visited in all of these years. Every day of my life I wonder why they left me and took all the other kids. What was so wrong with me?

The orphanage was a terrible place to live. Our beds were wet most nights because the roof leaked, the walls of the bedroom were black with mold, and it smelled bad all the time.

The only bathroom was outdoors, a hole in the ground. If it was snowing or raining, we still had to use it. The shower was also outside and had no hot water. In the summer we were allowed one shower a week, two girls at a time, for just a few minutes.

The oatmeal in the morning was cold, thin and never sweet. Lunch was a soup that was mainly water and a bite or two of carrot or potato. At night they would cook beans with some meat, removing the meat and leaving the fat.

They gave us just enough food to keep us alive.

We were all so thin. If we were late to a meal because of school or because we were sick, the workers would take our food and put it in buckets for their pigs, laughing at us as they did it.

I was always hungry.

Then one cold December day, God brought the Camerons into our lives. They came with hugs and smiles and laughter. The first time they came, we thought we would never see them again, but they kept coming back to see us every few weeks. It was amazing to think that they left their family in America to come help us orphans.

They fixed the heat, the roof, and installed toilets and showers inside the house. They built a real kitchen inside too. Before, the kitchen was outside and if it rained we would have to stand in mud up to our knees to get our food.

Dad (Philip) never missed a Christmas from the time he met us. He brought gifts and candies, he sang songs, and showed us in a thousand ways that he loved us. I didn't understand why he loved us, but he always came back.

In fact, one time he came just to give me a party on my birthday. Me—an orphan! It was the first cake I had ever eaten! I had never even heard of a birthday cake before!

When I was 16, I left the orphanage and never looked back. While so many other girls my age were dumped on the street with nowhere to go, I had a home and even better—a family. Stella's House was a dream come true. I had never seen such nice things. The furniture, the beds, the food! I could use the kitchen anytime I wanted! There were nice dishes and glasses!

And then the government gave the Cupcui Orphanage—the place I was raised in—to Dad. I wish I could say that I was happy at the news, but I never wanted to see that place again.

Before I knew it, all of us kids at Stella's House and Simon's House were asked to go out there on the weekends to clean, paint, set up furniture and make this place as nice as Stella's House for the children that would come.

I hated every single minute. I hated being there. Every room, every plate, every bed, brought back terrible memories. I could not wait to get back to Stella's House.

When we finally got permission to re-open the orphanage, we named it Providence House. And I thought I would never have to see that place again once it was opened. But Dad asked me to go out and help get the children settled. I didn't want to go, but I agreed. How could I refuse after the love he showed me? Then we started driving around picking up the children and I saw the conditions they were living in.

They were living in dirty, cold huts with no food for days. Their parents were drunks or abusive or both. They were crawling with lice and their shoes and filthy clothes didn't fit.

As we opened the door to Providence House and brought them inside, their eyes lit up, their smiles were amazing. They were so happy to be there!

I fell in love with each one of the children and now I don't want to leave Providence House! I lead church services for the children on Sundays, I brought home a newborn from the hospital, and I get to play and laugh in the very rooms I once hated so much.

Perhaps it doesn't sound like it makes sense—how I could love this place—but it is like Dad once explained to me: he has the love he has for me because God is in his heart. I have a love for these children and this place only because God is in my heart.

Valentina

Valentina D.
Orphaned at age of 19
Age today: 23

My name is Valentina.

I was the youngest of six children in a large and very poor family. At the age of one, my parents died and another family adopted me. We lived good days together and bad days. I always prayed to have a brother or a sister, but my new parents were told that they could not have kids.

One day God heard my desire and my stepmother got pregnant and gave birth to a boy when she was 42. All of us were very happy, and when he was born, we named him Andrei.

My life was full of joy. But then, my stepfather got sick and he died when my brother was only nine months old.

We became very poor after my stepfather died. I had to miss school a lot because I had to stay and take care of my little brother while our mom was working to make a little money so we would have something to eat.

That's how we lived for five years, then my stepmother, after working so hard all the time, got sick, too. In May 2009, she died.

I was totally destroyed. I could not think anymore. I felt that I was falling into a deep dark hole where I couldn't get out. I had no dreams and no hope. I was living but I didn't feel that I was alive, and I was thinking about my little brother. He was left with no parents at the age of five, and all these negative thoughts were pressing me down.

All I could think about was what I could to do help my brother... nothing of course. We both sat and cried for days. I had so many questions. What will I do next? How are we going to handle all the troubles?

I knew what happened to girls like me who didn't have any parents, any home—we either end up in the orphanage, or worse, we end up sex trafficked, forced to do horrible things with men who do not care about us at all. All they care about is themselves.

The tears would not stop. I was scared. I was scared I would become trafficked myself, or that I would be separated from my little brother. I thought that God did not exist, and even if he did exist He had forgotten us, but I was wrong.

One day my stepfather's cousin told me about an American man (Philip Cameron) who builds houses especially for orphan girls like me who had goals and dreams that were lost.

I decided to try and go to the city of Ialoveni where Stella's Houses are located. I couldn't take my brother with me, so I asked my aunt to take care of him for me. I showed up desperate for help at the gate of Stella's House. Philip Cameron and his family welcomed me with joy.

At Stella's House I met so many girls that were just like me. After talking to Philip Cameron I felt that something inside me moved. This man told me so much about God that I didn't know. I'm in University right now to become a clothes designer. I started to call Philip Cameron my father and Chrissie my mother. Now, they are taking care of my brother as well.

Here, I have discovered so much about God, and I'm born again. I look at the world different now. After knowing God, I realized that all these occurrences in my life were part of His plan for me. God lifted me up from that darkness, and He brought me back to life, a new life.

I lost parents two times but God took care of it all, and gave me another family with many sisters and brothers that I had always wanted.

Aurica

Aurica B.
Orphaned at age of 5
Age today: 18

My name is Aurica.

My mother and father never cared what happened to me or my sister. Mom left our village to find work and Dad locked us out of the house so he could get drunk. We had to beg the neighbors for food.

We never had a normal family. Our father is an alcoholic, and when I was five and my sister six, my father and my mother divorced.

When they divorced, Mom took us to our grandparents' house to live. I thought that this would be better. I thought that if we were away from our drunken father, he couldn't hurt us anymore. But our uncle lived there, too, and he did not like children.

For six years we lived with them. Like so many adults in my family, my uncle is an alcoholic, too—just like my father was. I thought I would be safer with my uncle, but he was single and he used to have wild parties with his friends all the time. He treated us like his slaves when his friends were around, making us do all the jobs for him, and cleaning up after them. If we didn't do whatever he was telling us to do, he beat us with a long stick.

We never had a good childhood because of my uncle and because we were the poorest children in the village. Everybody laughed and pointed fingers at us for the too small, ragged, dirty clothes that we used to wear.

In all those years living with my uncle, my mom only came once to visit us. That day, we told her that he was beating us, so she decided to put us in the orphanage. We lived in the orphanage for three years. I thought it would be better, that the people would be kinder. But the teachers told us that nothing was lower than an orphan.

I think after being there for so long, I started to believe them. What other choice did I have? My father was an alcoholic, and my uncle, the man who was supposed to take on a fatherly role, was just as bad as he was. The orphanage was the only place I could go. It was the safest place for me.

Every day, I feared what awaited me outside the orphanage. I knew I would be given enough money for a bus ride back home. Home, to where my uncle and father would beat me. The other scary thought was that I would wind up on the streets, and I knew what was waiting for me in the dark. Sex traffickers would take me and I would disappear.

But one day, Philip Cameron and his wife came to our orphanage and told us about Stella's House. When we entered this wonderful house, our world was completely changed.

For the first time, we felt that someone really cared about us and loved us. They were so kind to us, they became our family, and they gave us everything we needed. Because of their love, our eyes have been opened to God. We are so thankful for the people that God sent into our lives to help us.

Today, we know that Jesus is the Light. He changed our lives completely because He loves us.

Marina

Marina T.
Orphaned at age of 6
Age today: 18

My name is Marina.

I am the youngest of three children. I have an older brother and sister.

Our parents got divorced when we were very young and we were left with our alcoholic father who beat us all the time. He often left to work for two or three weeks at a time and would leave us locked in the house by ourselves, with no money to buy food.

But we were happy when our father wasn't around, because when he came back home, everything around us became dark. He would come home drunk and beat us all, kick us out of the house.

A lot of the times, we would sleep at our neighbor's house, and sometimes on the streets. After a while, our parents split us up, and my brother Artiom and sister Victoria went to stay with our mom, and I was left alone with my father. My father didn't want me to live with my mom, but he wasn't taking care of me either. His girlfriend beat me too, and didn't give me food.

One day, he gathered us all up and put us in the orphanage and forgot about us. At first, we were very happy because we thought that at the orphanage we would have a better life and nobody would beat us.

But at the orphanage, the conditions were very bad. At school, the teachers and workers treated us differently than the other children. We learned that to be an orphan is to be hated.

The roof at the orphanage was very old, and a lot of the times would leak inside. We didn't have showers inside or toilets. Our heater was very old and in the winter it was colder inside than it was outside. Everything was so old that it fell apart.

We would go to bed each night wondering if we would ever have parents that would love us and take care of us. We longed for someone to give us love, the hope that was missing in our lives.

One day we celebrated Christmas by singing to each other with no parents to listen. There were only a few teachers around but we knew they didn't want to be there. One man played along on an accordion, but the rest of the workers ignored us.

It was almost Christmas Day, but we had no presents. We never had any Christmas presents. We were about to finish singing our songs when the door opened and there was Philip Cameron. He walked in with a group of Americans and asked us if we could sing again.

Philip was the happiest person that we had ever seen. He was the first person to put a smile on our faces and tell us "I love you." He was the first person to give me a hug and make me feel special.

Philip changed our conditions at the orphanage, made everything new. Nobody ever suffered through cold nights or a cold shower again. He and his family spent days and days playing with all of us orphans and telling us who God is.

Then, when I was in grade seven, an organization in Moldova that is trying to put all the kids back with their families and close down the orphanages went to our father and offered him 15 chickens and 15 ducks to take us back.

Our father took the chickens and ducks, but as soon as the people were gone, he told us to go away. My brother Artiom, sister Victoria and I didn't know what to do, so we went to live with our mom at her apartment. A lot of the times, we didn't have food, or money to pay our rent and the lady who owned the apartment told us to leave. We didn't have money to buy clothes for school, notebooks, books, nothing.

It was the saddest, scariest time of my life. There was no hope.

One day we went to the market and there we ran into Philip Cameron. He was very happy to see us and he asked us where we were staying, how we were doing. I was sad to tell him we were hungry. Philip gave us money to buy what we needed that day.

Soon after, he asked us if we wanted to come to live at Stella's House. My brother, sister, and I were very happy. We wouldn't have to worry anymore about how we would pay our rent or how we would find food. We wouldn't have to worry anymore about what would happen to us all, if we would end up on the streets, scared and alone. My brother Artiom is in Simon's House now, and my sister and me are in Stella's House.

I don't know how to thank God enough for everything. Once we lived at the House, we started to hear more about God and the more we heard, the more we were hungry for God's Word.

God changed my life through Philip Cameron, gave me hope and a bright future. God gave me a bigger family than I had asked for. I started to call Philip and Chrissie Cameron Dad and Mom. God is my shield and hope and He is Alpha and Omega.

Natasha

Natasha G.
Orphaned at age of 7
Age today: 20

My name is Natasha.

When I was only two years old, my father walked out the front door of our house and out of my life forever.

The earliest memory I have was right after he left. It was raining outside and Mother had left me in the house for a moment to go draw water out of the well down the hill from the house. As soon as I realized I was alone, I panicked. I screamed and raced out of the house after her. I clung to her in the rain and cried and cried. I was so scared she would leave me, too.

The next memory I have is from when I was seven and my mother had a heart attack and died. My brother and I were left in the care of our grandparents. Grandmother was very kind, but we had nothing. There was never enough food to eat. We would try to help by stealing wood to burn in the winter to stay warm, but it was bitterly cold all winter.

My grandparents' house was large, but was all broken down. It was cold, there were holes in the floor and the windows were all broken.

We all had to work, even though I was just seven years old. I remember trying to farm the hills, trying to get some food to grow. There was no time to play. I had to weed and hoe everything.

No matter how hard I tried, things kept getting worse. They sold the cow. They sold things around the house just so we could live another day.

Then one day my grandfather took my hand and took my brother and me to the orphanage. I did not know what an orphanage was. I thought I might be going to school. I didn't know he was leaving us forever, my brother and me, alone with strangers.

Any hopes we had that there would at least be food didn't last. We were hungry all the time. The teachers were mean and when we upset them, they would take out long metal cables and whip us until we screamed.

I was so afraid at night; it was so dark. I would never go to the bathroom at night because I was too scared to go outside down the dark path to the place we had to go.

The day I aged out of the orphanage, I, like the other girls in the home, was given a bus ticket and $30 and was sent away from the only home I had known for most of my life.

I was terrified. As bad as the orphanage was, what awaited me in the world could have been so much worse. I had heard all the stories before, about girls who had aged-out and disappeared completely. Lots of people came to the orphanage with brochures and warned us about that.

They had no parents, no home, and no friends. They had no one who cared about them, and no one to know when they weren't around anymore. The scariest part was that now, the stories felt real. I was that girl with no one, scared that I might disappear, too. Was I going to be kidnapped and forced into the sex trade like so many others before me?

Thank God there was a bed for me at Stella's House—a dream too good to be true!

Only God knows what would have happened if there had not been a bed, but I am safe, I am happy, and I have a future much brighter than my past!

I am so overwhelmed that people who don't know me at all care about me enough to give me this wonderful life.

Dasa

Dasa R.
Orphaned at age of 7
Age today: 21

My name is Dasa.

Looking at my long hair, perhaps it is hard to imagine me trying to look like a boy. But for most of my childhood, I did try to be a boy.

You see, when my mother got pregnant, my father told her that he wanted a son. He wanted a son so badly that he told her if she gave birth to a girl, he would leave.

I wasn't a boy. My dad left right after I was born, so my mother blamed me. I tried and tried to act like a boy to win him back.

My early years were spent crammed into a small dirty house with little to eat and very little love. My first memory was of being marched outside and forced to kneel on hard dry kernels in the hot summer heat as punishment for whatever "bad" thing I had done. I must have been about four.

Every day as a child I woke up filled with fear. I saw my uncle throw boiling water on my little cousin. The terrifying sounds of my mother and/or one of my aunts being beaten savagely by my uncle woke me many nights.

I would put my hands over my eyes so I couldn't see what was happening, but I could still hear their screams.

"Please don't kill me," they begged.

Then one day, the violence stopped because my uncle was arrested as a thief and sent to prison. At first, life became more bearable and I began to have hope. But that soon ended. The remaining adults living in the home decided to leave the country for a "better life."

My mother and her sister left us children alone in the house for weeks at a time while they went to Russia to look for jobs. One of my older cousins came every few days with some rice to keep us alive. Without that rice, I would be dead today.

One terrible day, I was told that my mother had been in a car accident and was in a coma, clinging to life. I couldn't see her or go to help her. Instead, I was put in the state-run orphanage along with three of my cousins.

"You are nothing," the orphanage workers would mock us. "An orphan is less than nothing. You will never be anything."

Twice, I tried to commit suicide, but I couldn't even do that right. I was sad to wake up alive.

After nine miserable years in the orphanage, it was time for me to leave because I was 16—but I had nowhere to go. I had heard about Stella's House, but I didn't think there was room for me there.

Eighteen girls aged-out of the orphanage on the same day and we were all afraid of the same thing: disappearing. It was no secret what happened to girls who aged-out. They are taken, beaten and used by men again and again and again—all in one day. We would have even less than what we had in the orphanage, which was almost nothing already.

I was afraid to even pray for a dream like Stella's House. God had never heard me before. I felt I had no chance at the few beds because my mother was still alive so I am not an "actual" orphan. Plus I had learned to never trust anyone.

Everyone had failed me. These so-called Christians would be no different, I told myself.

But today, I trust Philip. He offered me a place at Stella's House and I know God and love Him now.

One day I want to open Stella's Houses in Africa or other countries. Everywhere the government runs an orphanage, they need homes like Stella's House.

No child should live the life I did. Everyone deserves to know God, to know love.

Daniela

Daniela L.
Orphaned at age of 9
Age today: 18

My name is Daniela.

I first met Philip when I was just nine years old. When he came to Cupcui, I was there with the other children, huddled together, trying to stay warm.

Over the years, Philip encouraged me to get better grades. He brought me and the other orphans warm clothes, boots, and Christmas gifts. But then, when the government shut Cupcui down, I was placed back with my family.

My mother agreed to take me back in exchange for a cheap wooden kitchen window. She had no way to take care of me, but she really wanted that window. I hated the orphanage, but I did not want to go back home.

One day, some medical people came to our village. They started giving medical exams to children to see if our lungs were healthy. Then, they visited my mom and told her that I had a four-and-a-half inch worm in my lung. I didn't have any pain in my lung, but they said they would remove the lung and the worm for free.

I was so scared when I went to the clinic. My mom told me having the lung removed was a good idea, so I went.

When I woke up, I hurt all over. There was a giant scar on my chest from where they had taken my lung. The doctors were gone. No one knew where they were, and I had only one lung.

Even after that, my mom would not let me go to school. She was so poor that she made me get a job working with machinery. I hated it there. I got paid only pennies a day, and the conditions were horrible. My boss screamed at me from morning until it was too dark to see at night, calling me names, telling me to work harder. I cried every day on my way to work and on my way home.

Then, one day, when I was working, my hand slipped. The sharp machinery sliced off half of my index finger. Blood was everywhere and I cried and cried.

Finally, some girls from Stella's House found me and took me to the House. They didn't have a room for anyone, but they set up a few beds in the basement for me and for some other girls who also needed a place to go.

When Philip came to visit, he was so happy to see me there. I went and sat with him and told him my story. He just sat and listened to me as I sobbed and sobbed. I had so much hurt, and so much to tell him about what had happened to me.

I am so happy to be here at Stella's House with Philip and the girls. I am starting to have hope again. I still cry, but I feel safe here, and protected.

Stela

Stela S.
Orphaned at age of 11
Age today: 19

My name is Stela.

My father tried to kill me many times. The first time he tried to kill me, I was only one year old. From the time I was five years old, he used to send me to bring him alcohol and if I did not bring it, he would beat me.

One day, he was making fun of me in front of his drinking buddies. He tied me to a table with a dog leash and laughed with the other men as I struggled to get away. When I finally got free, he broke my arm, but I escaped with my life, somehow.

As soon as I was out of his reach, I ran outside. I started running through the forest and cornfields. I didn't know what direction I was going but I knew my dad was behind me. After a long time running, suddenly I met up with my mom. She saved me from being killed that day.

For many years before that, my little brother and I used to hide under the bed when our dad came home drunk. Other nights, we would run away, sleeping in the cold cars, in the cemetery or on the streets.

I remember one night he demanded that we go out of the house, saying that the house was his, and we didn't have the right to stay there.

That night, my mom, my three brothers and I put our clothes in a paper bag and went to a neighboring village. It was 2:00 a.m., and we didn't have shoes on. Dad didn't care.

Many times my mom could not see how my father was abusing us because she was not home. She was often away selling something to make money for food and clothes. But when she brought things home for us, our dad sold them in exchange for alcohol.

Sometimes I would ask myself: Why was he so mean? What mistake have I done? Is he my father? He didn't act like a father. I had seen families where their father was kissing their kids, hugging them. I never got a hug from my father.

Finally, it got so bad that my mother thought that it would be better for us to go to an orphanage. We were relieved to be away from Dad, and thought we would finally be safe and happy. But the orphanage was terrible, too.

I was in the orphanage for five years, but for me it seemed like more. It was the same every day; there was nothing to look forward to. No reason for living.

Many Americans came in our orphanage and gave us stuff and told us that they loved us, but they went away and never came back. After they would leave, the workers at the orphanage would steal the gifts.

But when Philip and Chrissie Cameron came to our orphanage, they were not just giving us stuff; they became our Dad and Mom. I do not know how to explain the amazing work that they are doing in this country by supporting us. They are helping each of us to become someone.

They took me to Stella's House and showed me the right way to live. I have a room, a bed, a hot shower (which I never had), and food when I come home from school. I no longer live in fear that the people around me will take my things. I know that there will be food for me every day, and that I am safe here with my sisters, and I know that when Philip and Chrissie leave, they will be back.

The most important thing they brought was a light in my life, Jesus. Now I know that God will never leave me. He will never reject me because He is madly in love with me.

Ana

Ana J.
Orphaned at age of 5
Age today: 18

My name is Ana.

I know how to make people laugh.

But I was raised in the orphanage in Cupcui from the time I was five. Most of my life, there was very little to smile about.

One of my memories never leaves me. I see it over and over in my mind, like a movie that will not stop. The memory is there all the time—when I fall asleep, when I wake up—it is there.

I remember sleeping on the floor with my sister and hearing my father's angry voice. As he was many nights, he was drunk. This time, my mom had locked him outside the house. Loudly, he pounded on the door with his fist, screaming, demanding that my mother come out to him.

His voice, his actions, scared me to death. I didn't know what he would do. Finally, my mom opened the door and went out. I went to the window because I was scared for her, but it was so dark that I couldn't see much.

I could just barely see that she was lying on the ground, and he was kicking her. Over and over, he kicked, screaming how much he hated her. I could hear the dull thuds as he kicked and kicked her. She was crying, then whimpering.

And then she was quiet. Still, he kicked her. Finally, she just stopped moving.

Terrified, I ran out the back door and to my neighbors' house, begging them to come and stop my father from hurting my mother.

But the help was too late. My mother was left both physically and mentally handicapped for life from that beating.

After that terrible night, my sister and I were brought to the orphanage. Mom was so damaged that she turned to alcohol. She became drunk all the time to cope with her pain.

When Mom dropped us off at the orphanage, I tried to run after her, but the workers grabbed me and brought me back. I tried to fight back, crying, kicking. I wanted my mother, but no one cared.

Alone at the orphanage, I would dream at night and it was always of my mother before the beating. Her smiles. Her hugs. Her love. Then I would wake up and find myself still in that awful place. I would lie in bed and wonder how I could face another day without my mother.

One day, I met Philip Cameron. He was happy to find out that I knew English and asked me how I had learned to speak it. I had learned from watching television, as the workers kept the news on as they worked.

He told me that day if I made good grades in school, one day I could live in a wonderful house he had built for orphan girls. I did not believe him.

Yes, I knew he always brought toys and candies. I liked to talk with him. But his house was a dream I knew I could not have. Then last year, I was shocked when he came and took several of us to spend a day at the home—Stella's House.

I'll remember that day for the rest of my life. All the girls who lived there were smiling and happy. There were big plates of food and we could eat all we wanted. The rooms were big, clean, and so pretty.

It was not like any place I had ever been. I started to cry. I could not stop crying. I knew it was too nice for me to live at Stella's House. I was just an orphan. At the end of the day, I went back to the dreary orphanage, my sad world, and dreams of my mother.

Then, the workers told us that the orphanage was being closed and the government sent me back to my parents' house. Since I had been gone, my dad had become a better person, but my mother had turned into a mean drunk who no longer wanted to care for us. She threw knives at me and screamed at me, asking why I was there, over and over.

Thankfully, Philip found me and made a way for me to live at Stella's House.

Here, I have learned about Jesus, the Savior who loves me. I have a father and mother in Philip and Chrissie. I have so many brothers and sisters. I never really had a family before, but I do now.

I am in professional (vocational) high school, learning to sew with a career goal of fashion design.

When people come to Stella's House, I make them laugh with impersonations and jokes. I love to see their smiles. My joy is coming from my inside out.

Anna

Anna P.
Orphaned at age of 4
Age today: 18

My name is Anna.

When I was one and a half years old, my family went to a big party at a relative's house. At the end of the evening, my mother stayed behind and my father took me home and put me to bed.

The adults had been drinking, and no one fed us kids all night. In the middle of the night, I started to cry because I was so hungry. My father was mad that he was awakened, and when he realized my mother was not beside him in bed, he stormed out of the room looking for her.

He found my mother sleeping on the wooden stairs outside of my room. Furious, he picked up a wooden stick and began to beat her on the head. Blood was everywhere and still, he beat her and beat her with that stick. When he was finished, he pushed her with his foot and she rolled over against the wall.

"You better go to the hospital," he said, and then he went back to bed. My mother didn't go to the hospital, and three days later she was dead.

When she died, my grandfather took me to an orphanage for small children. My dad would visit me and there were times when a nice family would take me home for the weekend. I remember they would buy me clothes and food.

Once, when I woke up scared in the night, the nice couple let me sleep with them. It is my only good childhood memory.

When I got older, the state moved me to another orphanage across the country, and I lost touch with that family forever. From then on, I started guarding my heart.

I remember Philip coming to our orphanage, but I never talked to him. I would see him and just walk away. I didn't want my heart to be broken again.

During the summer, the orphanage would close and us children were forced to spend time with our parents when possible. Some of us had no family to visit, so the state would pay eleven cents a day to any family that would take me—or the other kids just like me—in.

One summer, I was placed with a family who made me work the farm all day. I milked the cows, weeded the garden and babysat their children. I was only a little girl, but they worked me from sun-up until it was too dark to see at night.

Then, another summer, my dad took me in and he seemed very glad to see me. Only days later, he changed.

He would wake me up every morning with a list of things he wanted me to do around the house, cleaning projects, meals he wanted me to prepare. He did not understand that in the orphans' home they did not teach us to cook or clean. I didn't know how to do what he was asking.

When I tried to tell him that I didn't know how to do the work, he would scream at me and slap my face. Once he threw a heavy metal can opener at my head. I was glad to escape him when summer was over.

Back at the orphanage, I began to hear about this place called

Stella's House. It seemed too good to be true. I was 15, so I knew my time was almost up at the orphanage, but I had nowhere to go.

One night at 2:00 a.m., someone knocked on my door and told me I had a phone call. I was frightened because no one ever called me—especially at this hour. Shaking, I picked up the phone to hear my father's unsteady breathing. I knew he had been drinking again.

"What are you doing?" he asked me.

"Sleeping. You?" I answered.

"I am watching pornography. Do you know what that is?" He then proceeded to describe in graphic, horrible detail what he was watching. I didn't know what to say, what to do.

He kept talking, then finished with words that made me tremble with fear and shame: "You keep your body pure for me, because when you get out of the orphans' home, you and I will be making babies together."

I hung up, shaking. The next morning, his words, his threat, were all I could think of. I tried to tell a teacher what happened, but she did not believe me. Finally, I told a friend who was living at Stella's House. She went to Philip and begged him to help me, to find me a bed at Stella's House and protect me from my father.

God is good. There was a bed open and they got me away from the orphanage the day I aged out and into safety. I would never have to go back to my father again. I feel safe here, away from my father, and away from the horrible orphanage.

The older girls of Stella's House were very protective of me. They talked to me about Jesus, about how He loves me and gave His life for me.

One day I will laugh and sing like the other girls; it is just a matter of time. I have already made the decision to ask Jesus into my heart. I often read my Bible quietly away from the others.

And I am warming up. It takes a while to begin to trust and to hope again. I have the time I need at Stella's House.

The Boys of Simon's House

"He who gives to the poor will lack nothing, but he who closes his eyes to them receives many curses."

(**Proverbs 28:27,** NIV 1984)

Radu

Radu C.
Orphaned at age of 8
Age today: 20

My name is Radu.

I was put in the orphanage in Ungheni because neither of my parents had jobs and the conditions were bad. My father saw that in Moldova there was no way find a job and went to Moscow, where he started to work and send money for us.

One year, on his birthday, he drank so much that he got in a car accident and died. For my mom, it was so difficult that she decided to put me in the orphanage and she went to find a job.

She went with gypsies to Romania, but it was still hard. She was coming to visit me at the orphanage and would say that she felt sorry that she had left me there. I told her that it was nothing and we would pass all this.

In the orphanage, my life was getting harder and harder because I lacked love. The teachers punished us for almost no reason. Sometimes I felt like a burden to them. I was silent and often went to my room and cried.

What I liked most was that all the kids encouraged each other and forgot what the teachers were telling us. As time passed, I needed more encouragements because of the fear I had. When I was about to leave the orphanage, the teachers were telling us the hardest time comes after the orphanage because we would not have anywhere to go and no way to pay for food and that the hardest time was coming soon.

But in the spring, a group of Christians came to our orphanage and told us about God. They did a Bible study with those who were staying in the orphanage for the weekend.

I felt amazing. It seemed like I was someone else. But, after they left, I went with the boys having parties and drinking alcohol and forgot everything that they told us. They were coming often to tell us about God, to teach us how to pray. I was trying. Something changed in me but I was not sure. I was not confident.

With only one month left to stay in the orphanage, I was thinking about where to continue my studies. I applied to a college and I was refused. For a year, I stayed home. My mom told me to try again and if I was rejected to find a job. I was so willing to learn.

I asked God for help. It did not work and God did not give what I asked for, so I told myself that it was a waste of time. I started to make trouble for my mom.

A year passed and a Christian friend of mine called me and asked if I wanted to continue in my studies. I asked him where I would be staying. He told me there was a house that helps boys, Simon's House.

I was accepted and attended school against all odds! I was so happy and from that day I started to believe that God exists and I realized that praying is not a waste of time. I apologized to my mom. My life now is changed. I feel a great love in my heart.

Today, I am so thankful to my two fathers, God and Philip Cameron. They gave me a new chance. Now I have a big family and feel so great being here. I am happy that God created me and blesses me so much.

Dima

Dima S.
Orphaned at age of 8
Age today: 17

My name is Dima.

When I was a little boy, my sister and I used to sleep outside in the garden, covering ourselves with leaves, hiding as best we could from our dad in the dirt.

He was a nasty drunk who beat my mother every night. My sister and I would run and hide so he would not hit us, too, but one day I decided to protect my mom. My dad beat me until I bled.

When I was eight, my sister and I were put in the orphanage. The kids were stealing from each other. The oldest boys took what little we had and then they beat us both.

I remember one night I felt sick and vomited on my pillow. The teacher that was staying during the night slapped me as hard as she could. I ran home to my mom, but she brought me back to the orphanage in the morning.

The teachers screamed and threatened me for running away. I was so scared, so alone, so hopeless.

In the orphanage some strange people came to tell us about Jesus.

I remember thinking, "This is not for me," and, "Why do I need this Jesus if my family has hurt me so much?"

When I was in seventh grade, my sister aged-out of the orphanage and went to Stella's House.

I wasn't sure what Stella's House was, but when she came back to visit she told me that Stella's House changed her and gave her the possibility to become someone.

I remember looking at her and thinking that this was impossible, because no one in this world helps you and if they help you they have a bad purpose.

After I finished the seventh grade, my sister came to the orphanage to see me again. She saw a Bible and started to ask my classmates and me questions from the Bible, and if we were reading it. As she shared, I saw how much she had changed. I saw hope.

The next year, she told me that there was a possibility for me to come to the house, because Dad (Philip) was opening a house for boys (Simon's House).

I was thinking, "Could this be true? Does God care enough for me to do this? Is Jesus really real? Does He exist?"

I was hoping I would be asked to go to Simon's House, but I had a problem. My record of behavior was not good and my grades were very low. I was so discouraged, but my sister was praying for me and telling me that God knows my heart.

Then a miracle happened. It was December 24 and my sister came to the orphanage and brought me to Simon's House. When I got there, they were celebrating Christmas.

There was a huge decorated tree, lots of food, and presents. I got the best gift of all. Jesus was my gift. He is a gift that never ends. I understand a lot more now and my life is changed completely. I want to encourage those that are reading my story. If there is something to do for God, don't stay and think, just do it. The results are amazing.

The Children of Providence House

For I was hungry and you gave me something to eat, I was thirsty and you gave me something to drink, I was a stranger and you invited me in, I needed clothes and you clothed me, I was sick and you looked after me... 'Lord, when did we see you hungry and feed you, or thirsty and give you something to drink? When did we see you a stranger and invite you in, or needing clothes and clothe you?'...The King will reply, 'Truly I tell you, whatever you did for one of the least of these brothers and sisters of mine, you did for me.'

(Matthew 25: 35–40, NIV)

Igor

Igor F.
Orphaned at age of 11
Age today: 13

My name is Igor.

I am so thin, looking at me, you would think I am only eight years old, but I am really 13.

After living at Providence House for a few weeks I took off on my own. I had enjoyed living in a warm home, sleeping in a real bed for the first time in my life, owning a change of clothes, and knowing that there would always be another meal in a few hours...

But a few hours before the Christmas party I left and returned to a dirty, cold house where there was nothing to eat.

My 90-year-old grandmother was sick with cancer. Her home has no electricity or running water. The only heat she has comes from a log on the fire, but she is too sick to look for wood and too poor to pay for it, so she doesn't have a fire very often.

Living in this same house is my uncle. Every day he leaves, finds enough money to get drunk, and then comes home and beats my poor grandmother before passing out.

I want to protect my grandmother. I love her so much. Philip came looking for me the night I left Providence House; he knew why I had left and he knew where to find me.

He sat me down and held my hand. I remember his eyes were full of tears as he explained: my mother had run away to Russia, my grandmother was very ill, and my uncle would hurt me. He knew I wanted to protect my grandmother, but he told me that I can't— I do not have the strength to help her. But if I chose to live at Providence House, I would be safe and loved.

It was so hard for me. I wanted to do the right thing. And I wanted to have a real family.

I asked him if I could call him Dad.

He hugged me. I don't think anyone had ever hugged me like that. I cried and clung to Philip—Dad—for the longest time.

Later, he told me not to worry about missing the big Christmas celebration. The night I had run away, he had saved his gift for me! I was filled with such happiness as I ripped open a box containing toy cars, a ball, a new sweater, and coloring books.

I may have missed the Christmas party at Providence House, but I won't miss another celebration! I am home.

Irina

Irina C.
Orphaned at age of 7
Age today: 20

My name is Irina.

I met Philip when I was a little girl at the Cupcui Orphanage before he did any repairs there. Like the other children, I was very, very thin, almost starved to death. I had been sick for as long as I could remember.

Somehow, I managed to stand out among the sea of sad faces Philip and Chrissie found there.

While all the other children had features much like any Eastern European, my skin, my almond-shaped eyes, and jet-black hair, all gave me the look of a priceless doll, they told me. Their words were like music. Chrissie and Philip fell in love with me and they even tried to adopt me.

All seemed clear for them to adopt me when a hunchbacked man with greasy white hair and a look of pure disgust on his face walked into the orphanage.

He would have been impossible to forget. It was my grandfather. He leaned hard on one side with a wooden stick while raising his other dirty hand right in Philip's face.

"You'll not take her!" he snarled. "You'll not." And with that, he poked that grimy finger into Philip's chest.

We could tell he had been drinking heavily and would either fall dead on the floor or go after Philip with his makeshift cane.

"I said, you'll not take her. Irina. She belongs to me," my grandfather continued.

My mother lived with her father—my grandfather—and he had beaten us almost to death years ago. It was his decision to put me in the orphanage, not because he cared, but because he didn't want to share what little food he had with me. I was a skinny girl, too young to be of any help in the garden. He had no need for me now.

Not now, but he told Philip, "Soon I am going to be an old man. Someone will have to care for me. I'll come back and get her then; she'll be older and worth something."

Think of it: the only thing on his mind was having someone to look after his own selfish needs.

He yelled again, shaking that boney finger at Philip.

"I've heard about your types. Think I don't know what you are up to? You want to take her away where no one will ever hear from her again. You'll sell her for body parts. Her eyes, her heart, her lungs, who knows what? You are a bad man. Stay away from Irina. My Irina."

Chrissie and Philip said they wept for days over me. By the time of their next visit, I was gone. They checked at my grandfather's house and with my neighbors in the village.

All anyone knew was when I turned 16 and aged-out of the orphanage, there was a boy waiting for me. I thought he was my boyfriend. I walked out of the orphanage with all my belongings in a small paper bag, and disappeared into the night with him. I thought a happy life was ahead of me. But I was wrong. Nothing good waited for me outside of the orphanage.

The entire time I was gone, Chrissie and Philip never stopped looking for me, praying for me, calling my name before the Lord.

Then a few weeks ago, Galina called Philip with the news.

"Dad?" Galina almost shouted into the phone, "Dad, it's a miracle! Dad, Irina...she is here...right beside me. She came back!"

The rest of the story spilled out through Galina's tears. My "boyfriend" was nothing but a liar—he had one use for me, and that was to sell me to as many as 20 men a night.

My Asian features made me a novelty, and therefore, even more popular. I only survived by literally going out of my mind. I was thrown into a mental hospital, and when I started showing the signs of pregnancy, I was kicked out of there, too.

It took days to get there, but I returned to the only home I'd ever known, the orphanage at Cupcui. What I didn't know was that Philip's ministry now ran it, had completely refurnished it, and renamed it Providence House. Their arms were open to desperate pregnant girls. I know they'd give help to any girl—but especially me.

I am so glad to finally be safe, and to have a loving place to raise my baby. I really am home.

Svetlana

Svetlana S.
Orphaned at age of 7
Age today: Unknown

My name is Svetlana.

I was very poor and was lured by the promise of a job selling leather jackets in Italy. The men lied to me, and I wound up being trafficked in Turkey. When I reached my destination, I was led to a small hotel room crowded with other young girls my age.

One of them told me I had been sold and I would have to be a prostitute. When the man came back to the room I asked him to please let me go. Before he would let me go, he told me I would have to repay him what he paid to get me. He then asked if I had 1,500 Euros.

Of course, I did not, so he grabbed me by the arm and dragged me down the hallway and into an empty room. I started to scream for mercy. I told him I was a virgin, begging him to let me go.

Rather than show me mercy, the man increased my price and my virginity was sold for 100 Euros to the first man who offered the money.

When I woke up from the attack, I wished I were dead. I hurt all over from the beatings and from the rape. I played it over and over again in my head.

And it didn't stop. Night after night, day after day, men would come to my door and force me to do the unthinkable.

In time, I learned to numb the pain—with no money and no one to help, I thought I would never escape. But one day, I met a hotel employee who helped me escape! When I went to take out the trash, he drove up and swung the car door open. I dropped the garbage and leapt inside the car and we sped off to the Embassy where I began crying and telling my story to officials.

Later, I met Philip. He and Chrissie had a spare single room at Providence House and once he heard my story, he offered it to me.

Two months later, I gave birth to a sweet little girl named Maria. But there is still so much hurt in my heart. I am still very angry, and it is hard for me to look people in the eye. I am afraid that they will hurt me like all of those men did, because I have already bought the lie that I am nothing but a worthless piece of meat, good only to be used by men.

EDITOR'S NOTE: Svetlana left Providence House with her baby after many emotional, violent outbursts. Her pain was so great, her heart so guarded, and we were unable to help her. We pray for her every day.

The Truth About
Sex Trafficking

*"Speak up for those who cannot speak for themselves,
for the rights of all who are destitute. Speak up and judge fairly;
defend the rights of the poor and needy."*

(Proverbs 31:8-9, NIV 1984)

I spend many nights alone away from my beautiful wife in hotels as I travel the world sharing the Gospel.

The human side of me can, on some level, understand why some men who have no relationship with the Lord, or no morals, reach out to prostitutes when they are far from home and believe their families will never find out. A willing girl, an exchange of money, and the deed is done; life goes on.

But for the life of me, I cannot figure out what is attractive about having raw sex with a girl who is visibly drugged, beaten, and being used against her will. Girls who are trafficked do not fit the prostitution stereotype often portrayed in movies and on television; they are not there for any other reason than because they are forced to be.

Every minute, one victim is trafficked across international borders.[1] That means that right now, as you read these very words, someone is being stolen, forced into the worst imaginable life.

I was shocked, disgusted, and most of all, heartbroken to learn that there are 27 million people enslaved around the world today. Not even the Trans-Atlantic slave trade saw that many slaves in the 400 years that it existed![2]

According to the Polaris Project, sex trafficking is a $32 billion industry annually, and half of that total is made in industrialized countries[3]—countries like the United States, the United Kingdom—countries we think of as civilized.

But how can we call our countries civilized when every minute, women are being stolen, beaten, raped over and over again?

---

[1] "Innocents at Risk—The Facts," Innocents at Risk, accessed March 28, 2013. http://www.innocentsatrisk.org/human-trafficking/the-facts.

[2] "Human Trafficking," The Polaris Project, accessed February 11, 2013. http://www.polarisproject.org/resources/resources-by-topic/human-trafficking.

[3] Ibid.

"In Europe alone, officials estimate that more than 200,000 women and girls... are smuggled out of Central and Eastern Europe and the former Soviet republics each year, the bulk of whom end up working as enslaved prostitutes."[4] Even here in America, the supposed beacon of freedom for this world, 300,000 women and children are sold into slavery each year.[5]

Without these sick men, there would be no market for the sex trade. If there were no easy market for these girls, the traffickers would move on to something else besides peddling flesh.

All of this makes me ashamed to be a man. How could they? They say the top three reasons men pay for sex are: they have an urge, they have a specific fetish, or they are unsatisfied with their relationship.

I'll give you my thoughts on what the top three reasons are:

First, the enemy seeks to destroy as many lives as possible, and sex outside the covenant of marriage is a sin of the body that affects both women and men forever. The Bible tells us in 1 Corinthians 6:18 to *"Flee from sexual immorality. All other sins a person commits are outside the body, but whoever sins sexually, sins against their own body."*

Second, we live in an "it's all about me" world. People want what they want regardless of what it does to someone else, and people take what they want to take. *"You desire but you do not have, so you kill. You covet but you cannot get what you want, so you quarrel and fight"* (James 4:2, NIV). Men see these girls, and they take them because they want to take them. How can a man call himself a man when he would so easily take a girl and rape her, simply because he wants to?

And third, sin is progressive. Ask any recovering addict. You start small to get a kick from it. Then it takes more and more to get you the

---

[4] Mendenhall, Preston. "Infiltrating Europe's Shameful Trade in Human Beings," National Broadcasting Company, accessed February 11, 2013. http://www.nbcnews.com/id/3071965/#.UVSj4o7C4uI.

[5] "Innocents at Risk—The Facts," Innocents at Risk.

same buzz. Men that will take and use an enslaved 15-year-old girl didn't start there and the next time, they will want to do something even more grotesque. *"Each person is tempted when he is lured and enticed by his own desire. Then desire when it has conceived gives birth to sin, and sin when it is fully grown brings forth death"* (James 1:14-15, NIV).

God put it into my heart years ago to do everything I could do to protect these girls from the evil that awaits them, to care for and love these children. I cannot stand idly by and watch as thousands of girls age out of orphanages across Moldova with nowhere to go.

If we can stop it in Moldova—and we can—we can stop it anywhere.

Afterthought

(Andrew)   (Natalie)

Once upon a time, there was an orphaned boy named Andrea (Andrew), abandoned in a god-forsaken orphanage in Romania. He was left alone in his filthy crib, night and day, touched only when he was changed. To comfort himself, he would stand in the bed, hands gripping the railings, and rock back and forth, clanking against the cribs on either side of him.

In nearby Moldova, there was an abandoned girl named Natalie (see page 13). Every Saturday, from dawn until dusk, she stood at the gate of the orphanage, hoping and praying that her mom would come to visit. Weeks turned into months, months turned into years, and her mother never came. And yet, Natalie still waited.

She waited every Saturday, in the rain, the snow, the heat, the cold—whatever the weather—until one day she learned that her mother had been to the orphanage. In fact, she had been there just the day before. She had come with her new boyfriend to see his kids, but never walked down the hall to ask for Natalie.

As sad as her life was in the orphanage, as she neared her sixteenth birthday, she dreaded what would come next.

She had nowhere to go. She had no way to make an income.

These two orphans, Andrew and Natalie, impacted my life in such a profound way. Andrew, I adopted and raised from the time he was four. Today, he is a young man, full of God's spirit, college-educated, with a heart for orphans. He is my son.

Natalie was one of 18 girls I found lined up one sunny June morning on a bench in front of the orphanage. They had just completed their last duties as orphans: to make their rooms ready for the next kids. Natalie and the others were covered with paint.

"Do a good job," the workers would sneer as the girls worked, "one day your children will be here."

I was told that overnight these 18 girls would be sent away, each with a mere $30 and a bus ticket to the village she was born in.

At the time, we only had one Stella's House built. It was full, but there was one room we kept open as a place for the girls to study.

Turning to my wife, I asked, "How many beds would fit in that room?"

Three, I was told. Just three. I looked at the 18 faces. The three we picked would be educated, loved, protected and introduced to a God that loves them. The others? Trafficked? Starved on the streets?

How could I possibly pick? I couldn't. Finally, I asked the girls at Stella's to help me. They chose Natalie and two others. The rest slipped through my fingers and into the cruel world.

But Natalie, a girl I didn't know until that day, with her dazzling smile and warm gentle eyes, came to us that day as a frightened, battered shell of a girl. But from her first week at Stella's House, she opened her heart to our love, and to the Jesus we serve. That alone was a miracle.

She worked harder than I could have ever dreamed, mastering English with no formal training. Her schoolwork was excellent, and she soon became a vital part of the Stella's Voice family.

As time went on, she became one of the girls whose faith exploded and her gifts became evident. She could lead worship! She could lead Bible study! Her progress was staggering.

One summer, I brought her and several other girls to the States to minister and share in churches across America. Everywhere she shared, lives were changed.

She and the other girls stayed with my wife and two daughters all summer, in the sleeping quarters that we had added to our attic.

I guess I should have seen it coming, but I was blindsided. Between church services, road trips and pizzas, Natalie caught the eye of Andrew—or vice versa.

On August 31, 2012 my son Andrew married my "daughter" Natalie in a service I will never forget. (It is still online if you'd like to watch!) And yes, they will live happily, eternally.

But what of the other 15 girls on the bench? In the years that have passed, we found just one. The rest are lost to us forever. I am sure each had a childhood as painful as any you have read. And now they face even worse.

Right now, I have a building project underway that will provide housing for another 60 girls just like Natalie, like the others on these pages. I need to find 1,000 people that will send $100 to continue our

work and raising support for the next phase. Any amount will help; perhaps you can give $1,000 or even $500?

If these stories have moved you in any way, please help. Be the bridge to a future for countless girls and boys just like them. Give as generously as you can.

Every single dollar helps more than you know. It is the difference between an orphan being **sold or saved**.

By the Numbers

What do these number mean?

27
400,000
$32
98
2,000
12.3
161
57,000
200,000

I'll tell you what they mean:

27 million[1]—Number of people that the Polaris Project reports are in modern-day slavery around the world.

400,000[2]—Estimated number of women and girls that have disappeared from Moldova since 1989.

$32 billion[3]—Total yearly profits, in U.S. dollars, that the Polaris Project reports is generated by the human trafficking industry.

98[4]—Percent of victims who are women or girls.

---

[1] "Human Trafficking," The Polaris Project, accessed February 11, 2013. http://www.polarisproject.org/resources/resources-by-topic/human-trafficking.

[2] "Former Orphans Bring Hope to Troubled Children," Philip Cameron Ministries, accessed February, 11 2013. http://www.philip-cameron.org/news/former-orphans-bring-hope-to-troubled-children/.

[3] "Human Trafficking," The Polaris Project.

[4] *Ibid.*

2,000[5]—A human trafficker can receive up to 2,000 percent profit from a girl trafficked for sex.

12.3 million[6]—Number of men, women and children that are trafficked for commercial sex or forced labor around the world today.

161 countries[7]—Trafficking affects 161 countries worldwide.

57,000[8]—Number of Moldovans who become victims of human trafficking each year.

200,000[9]—Estimated number of women and girls who are trafficked out of Central and Eastern Europe and the former Soviet republics each year, the majority of whom end up working as sex slaves.

---

[5] "Human Trafficking Statistics," Justice for Youth, accessed February, 11 2013. http://www.justiceforyouth.org/human-trafficking-statistics/.

[6] "Trafficking in Persons: Ten Years of Partnering to Combat Modern Slavery," US Department of State, accessed February, 11 2013. http://www.state.gov/r/pa/scp/fs/2010/143115.htm.

[7] "Human Trafficking," The Polaris Project.

[8] Ukraine's Human Trafficking Statistics for 2006," Try Ukraine, last modified February, 28 2007. http:// www.tryukraine.com/news/2007/07.shtml.

[8] Mendenhall, Preston, "Infiltrating Europe's shameful trade in human beings," accessed February, 11 2013. http://www.nbcnews.com/id/3071965/#.UVnKbI7C4uJ.

What You Can Do

*"A generous man will himself be blessed,
for he shares his food with the poor."*

(Proverbs 22:9, NIV 1984)

You can help us stop sex trafficking in Moldova! With your help, we can provide safe, loving, Christ-filled homes for aged-out orphan girls in Moldova. Next June, another group of innocent girls will be sent away from the state-run orphanage. Help us do more, save more. Help us to build a place for them and give them a bright future.

Here's what you can do:

1) **Make a donation.** Visit www.stellasvoice.org/donate to give a gift today.
2) **Join a prayer group.** Please pray for us as we pray for you. We invite and encourage you to send in your prayer requests. Each will be prayed over and your need lifted to the Father by name.
3) **Start a gift drive.** We need new coats, boots, toys, non-perishable food items, and much more. Visit www.stellasvoice.org/join to learn more.
4) **Take a missions trip.** Change a life while you change your own! Take a group to Moldova and spend your days ministering to children and teens that have grown up hearing they are worthless.
5) **Start a fundraising page for Stella's Voice.** It's simple and will reach people who have never heard of Stella's Voice. Use your social media platform to make your voice even louder for the orphans in our care and for the ones we have yet to reach with the love of Jesus Christ. Go to www.stellasvoice.org/donate/start-a-fundraiser for step-by-step instructions.
6) **Share this book or our 30-minute video** (http://vimeo.com/31929615) with your friends, family, and especially your pastor. Help us get invited to come and share. Some of our girls are in the States for most of the year. Their English is nearly perfect; their ministry gifts beyond measure. Contact Andrew Cameron (yes, *that* Andrew) at acameron@stellasvoice.org.
7) **Give the orphans a better chance for a better life.** By doing any or all of these things, you are changing the lives of every orphan currently in our care, and any orphan who comes into our care in the future.